This book is dedicated to my sibling.

I could not have been here without

them.

Therefore, I could not have done any

of this without them.

Thank you to my mother, my

grandmother and my grandfather as

well for supporting me in my journey

through school and on this wonderful

journey into writing.

I hope everyone enjoys this short

journey into my poems.

Panic Attack

Agitated, barely breathing,

Ailment overcoming my body,

Alarms sounding, heart pounding,

Angry words spewing hatred, piercing

my body,

Growing faint, failing to comprehend

the surroundings,

Grabbing my chest, lights fading out,

Heart failing to function,

Heat flowing through my body like an

uncomfortable sauna,

Head losing all thoughts, lights

completely gone now.

Why?

Why force it,

When nothing is there?

Enjoyment vanished,

Love is elsewhere.

Why choose it,

If it is not wanted?

Forcing a smile,

Taking it in.

Why leave it,

If it is needed?

Causing unhappiness,

Smirk creeping from another.

Narcissism

Disease creates
Unmedicated perfection.
Rips through a family,
One by one,
Til all that's left is one,
One parent,
one child.

Disease creates
A scared child.
Piecing together the world,
All alone.
Caring for a parent,
Not being a child,
Scared and lonely.

Disease creates
A horrified teen.
Searching for answers,
Coming up short every time.
Looking for help,
Being the problem,
And finally feeling at home.

In Sickness and In Health

Picking up the pieces of your mess,

Not bothering with the rest.

Can't connect with your eyes,

Won't even be mad about your lies.

Shattered glass and stained rug,

All you wanted was a hug.

Broke apart in your arms,

Heard the alarms.

Cleaning the house,

Crying into that blouse.

Picking myself up,

Only to see another broken cup.

Perfection

Clearly worn from use,

I stand ready for my next assignment.

I am always ready for whatever I am

assigned,

Standing tall and eloquent.

Sometimes I am assigned a simple,

easy task.

I will find myself filled with simple

brown earthy tones.

Other times, the task is difficult and I

am unsteady.

I may be forced to use greens or

another bright color,

which could take weeks to wash out

completely,

I still need to work the same as before.

It is my job to make sure everything is

blended to perfection.

The brighter the color, the more I have

to blend.

I have never turned down a challenge,

This is why I am kept so neatly in my

place.

I have seen many others fall to the

back or never seen again

If their assignment was not completed

to absolute perfection.

Growth?

Cold, tired, hungry, surrounded,

Never alone.

Rushing without wanting,

Not having control.

Clean, full, warm, surrounded,

Never alone.

Smart and eager,

Willing to learn.

Restless, but surrounded,

Sometimes alone.

Looking for new,

Coming up empty.

Tired, warm, in love,

Not feeling alone.

Finally free,

Started a family tree.

Exhausted, starving, confused,

surrounded,

But feeling alone.

Autopilot days and nights,

Losing all control.

Love Me

Changing places,

Peering into my eyes,

I see who you see,

I see her.

Empathy fading,

Desperation flourishing

In the bright blue iris

Of a blue girl.

True desperation triumphs,

Praying only to leave,

So to never be left,

Still hoping this love can truly be.

The End

Bright light flickering,

Ground breaking underneath me.

Reality fading,

But this is true.

Light breaks through me,

Only to fade into darkness.

People have disappeared,

I've faded now.

Life

I was born to a loving mom that ALWAYS wanted me to be the best. She had big plans for me. I would be a doctor, a lawyer or in any other extremely prestigious profession. I started talking at the age of one and haven't stopped since. I have always been able to talk a person's ear off. I was also that three year old who would sit in the bathtub playing educational games. I was that three year old child who would read and write and do workbook activities. My parents had always pushed me. I went to an elementary school that was literally called "Ivy League". Yeah, I know, prestigious right? I never had an issue with schoolwork. I however, did seem to find leaving my parents very difficult, well my mom at least. I was never close with my dad until much later on, then we became estranged again. I was very advanced in school and went into Kindergarten at 4 years old

My Sibling Story

I have a younger sibling who was in and out of the hospital since they were two weeks old. I had always worried about them and will always worry about them. When they were two weeks old, my mom had found out that my sibling has a heart condition. The doctors had never seen anything like it. When they took one look at my sibling, they told my mom that they couldn't be sick. I've seen the other sick little kids and my sibling just never looked like that. Which, in my opinion, makes it even worse. No one could know they were sick unless they did extensive testing, which, in fact, they did. The doctor finally did extensive testing on them and after this, had told my parents to go home and spend as much time with my sibling as they could because my sibling wouldn't have more than a few weeks left, if that. They were dead from the waist down. Through the most amazing surprise and present me or my parents could have ever gotten, my sibling's cardiologist was a most arrogant man. He was not ready to give up. As soon as the nurse said there was nothing they could do, this man took the challenge. He said he can do anything, and in fact, he could. I could never thank that man enough for what he did for my entire family. My sibling was fixed, well, for the most part. They still had and always will have a heart condition, but they were going to live on.

My One True Wish

My grandfather was ripped away from me at the age of four. He was extremely young. A heart attack. A heart attack. That's how my strong grandfather died. He died where no one could help him. He loved me. He loved me beyond compare. I was so close with him when I was only four years old. This man was so proud of me through everything that a little four year old could do. On my second birthday, this was the man that I walked to. We both felt that bond; the bond that I still feel. I know that he's dead, but it still feels as though he's here with me sometimes. I feel his presence a lot. It might be odd, but I still need him in my life and I'm not ready to give him up just yet. Some young kids have imaginary friends, I just pretended that my grandfather was still with me. I know it's not possible, but he's the one thing I wish for. Every single birthday, whenever I can wish on a candle or a star, I wish that he can be here with me. I've been doing this ever since he died. Even at my sweet sixteen, the one thing I wished for while blowing out the candles was that my grandfather could be here to celebrate it with me. He wasn't there for my sweet sixteen. I still gave him a candle, but of course, he wasn't able to receive it and I cried through the whole thing. He won't be able to see me walk down the aisle on my wedding day. He wasn't able to take me out to lunch or dinner or protect me against boys. He wasn't able to protest boyfriends or anything like that. He never got to know me, but I just hope that he'd be proud of who I became since he died. I hope that he knows that I strive to make him proud.

The Worst Crime

Rape. This concept has multiple different connotations. To me, this meant my innocence was gone. No more being a little girl. That was over. No more trusting people. I can't. My cousin. Someone I was supposed to trust and share hair braiding tips with, had in fact, ripped my innocence away. I was five years old. I had no idea what this meant or what was happening to me. Considering these facts, I didn't know how to tell anyone what was happening and I didn't know how to stop it. My cousin had convinced me that this was something that was supposed to happen. Through the five year old mind that I held, I believed her. It somehow made sense to me. Yes, I told her to stop. No, I didn't know what was happening to me and no I didn't tell anyone what was happening to me. I suppressed this feeling and memory that I had until much later down the line. At the age of 16, I had somehow remembered what had happened for the first time since I was 5. I had no idea how to handle it. I felt completely embarrassed and ashamed. Yes, I knew it wasn't my fault, but even still, I was embarrassed and I still am quite embarrassed. She was a girl. You hear of guys raping girls, but you never hear of girls raping girls. She also was only a couple years older than I was. It's a confusing topic, but it still hurts and most likely always will. It feels worse that I have to be embarrassed that my rapist wasn't some 50 year old man. It was a young girl. How many people can say that? Probably not too many. Since that memory came back to me, I have not been able to trust really anyone. I can't even trust some of my family. How sad is that? I'm completely embarrassed. What am I supposed to say when I'm ready to have that experience with some guy that I really like? He won't be my first. My first time was forced on me. My virginity was ripped away from me and I had no say in it. I can't have it back and how am I supposed to tell someone that? I feel like damaged goods. This is a struggle that most people who were raped feel. Believe me, I have talked to a few of them.

However, I Was Saved

I went from a home where everything and everyone was neglected to a home where everything didn't just look perfect, but was perfect, overnight. I went through multiple counts of mental and emotional abuse and neglect. Due to his firm disbelief in doctors, my father has never been diagnosed with anything formally. However, when working through in therapy the emotional and mental trauma that he has put me through over the years, I have never found a therapist that hasn't been able to come up with the conclusion that my father is a severe narcissist and a pathological liar. Now, this makes every single argument I have with him- every single restless night - that much worse. The thing about narcissists and pathological liars is that not only are their arguments completely self-serving, but their arguments have no logical reasoning behind their thought process - they are simply just lying through their teeth.

I remember when I was still living with him, we had no money because he felt that his time was too valuable and he didn't want to work. My mom had about two or three jobs at the time, I can't exactly remember, but was still expected to put food on the table, do homework with two children and raise them all by herself because yes - he didn't help out. I was six or seven years old at the time; so obviously I was growing constantly.

We were so poor to the point where I

was wearing clothes that noticeably

could not fit me - and I don't mean are

too tight - I mean would show a little

belly. Therefore, my grandparents felt

the need to take their granddaughter on

a shopping spree to get just a couple of

outfits that fit her - enough at least for

the school week and then, of course, I

would be made fun of for re-using the

same clothes. Anyways, being forced

to live with that and feeling obligated

to go back and forth between his and my grandparents' houses when my parents finally split, it was a lot of trauma on a little girl. However, I was saved.

My True Hero

A hero is not some fictional character that saves masses of people. A hero is someone who goes through their normal life not even knowing how much they've touched the lives of people they love. A hero is someone who doesn't know they mean that much to anyone. A hero doesn't think they've made that much of an impact on anyone, but without realizing it, they created a reason for someone to live another day.

Most people think of Superman, Spiderman, Ironman or some other superhero when asked who a hero is. For some reason, I have never thought that way. I feel as though a hero is someone who works through every struggle and breaks through stronger than they could have ever imagined. Of course, a hero doesn't have to be defined by someone who never struggles.

I've been lucky enough to have a few of these heroes in my life. A few honorable mentions are my mother who never gave up hope on creating the best life for her two daughters. Another one is my sister who has been through more in her fifteen years than any person could even fathom in their forties or fifties. However, a true hero that hasn't got enough credit over the years is my grandmother.

A hero is someone who pushes through the tough times in their lives and creates a better life for their loved ones. My grandmother didn't have an easy life, but a hero doesn't have to. My grandmother has never failed to find a place in her home or her heart for any of her grandchildren. I know that she loves all of her grandchildren, but I truly believe that I am one of the luckiest people in the world because I get to live with my grandmother.

My grandmother isn't perfect, because a hero can't be. However, my grandmother does her absolute best to make sure I always feel perfect. My grandmother doesn't even begin to grasp the fact that she's the reason I am who I have become these past few years. My grandmother will always humble herself and say that I did it all myself but everyone knows that those nights where I didn't know what I was doing with my life, my grandmother was there to say every single thing that I needed to hear.

My grandmother only speaks highly of her grandchildren and makes sure that every single one of us feels as though we are perfect and loved more than we know. My grandmother doesn't care if she gets anything in return for all of the amazing things she has done for all of us; she just wants us to be the very best version of ourselves.

My grandmother has never let me feel an ounce of pain if she knew about anything that hurt me. She had always tried to make every situation better and she still does, even though I'm turning twenty this year. She doesn't know an age; she just knows that the second I need her, she's there.

A true hero doesn't have crazy superpowers and they don't save cats from trees. A true hero has this amazing superpower called love. My grandmother has never made me feel as though I was unloved. In fact, my grandmother makes it a habit to say that she loves me just about every day, sometimes multiple times a day.

I think the true heroic thing that a hero could do is just be there, and that's one thing that my grandmother excels at. I could call her from a million miles away and just say "Gammy, I need you," and I could bet a million dollars that she would find a way to be there as soon as it was possible. My grandmother has been there through all of my struggles and I wouldn't have wished for anyone else to be there for me.

The most important thing that my grandmother has done for me is she has this crazy superpower that allows her to say every single thing that I need to hear at any given moment. She has kept me from jumping off the ledge quite a few times, and the craziest thing is that she doesn't even know it. She has no idea the impact that she's made on my life; she just loves me unconditionally and continues to say all of the right things. For this, my grandmother will always be my favorite superhero.

A Little Blue Box

When the commotion starts, I know it's time to turn my brain off. I look to my left and open my little blue box and stare into the emptiness before entering my escape.

I wake up in what seems to be a black hole. I crawl around blindly until I feel a light switch. Suddenly, I see I'm in a hospital room. I jump off of the bed and reach for the door, which leads to a ginormous staircase. At the top of these stairs, is a never ending hallway lined with hospital rooms,

filled with children. I enter the first

room and begin checking the patient's

vitals. I carefully look at the infant's

startled face and feel guilt, as if

something I'm doing is wrong. I notice

the mother anxiously staring at her

newborn baby. Upon finishing, I make

a point to look towards the mother and

smile. I feel there's never an escape;

every room is filled with sobbing

adults and confused children.

Instinctively, I move on to the next

room. After meeting my new patient, I feel the room start to spin.

"Adelaide! Adelaide!" I empty out my blue box and slam it shut before my mom enters my room.

"I was calling you for ten minutes, what were you doing?" My mom questions me from my door frame.

"I was studying," I look up at her and force a smile.

The next morning, I open my blue box, knowing it's cleaned out, and feel myself slip back into a dream.

I wake up to the sound of my pager. I hate being on call; I always know as soon as I try to fall asleep, I'll be called back in.

I rush to the hospital and find one of my regular patients sitting in the waiting room. While I don't mind catching up with my patients, I would much rather do so in a happier setting. I look over at his father who has his head in his hands. I glance over at the desk and see the nurse instantly look down, attempting to break eye contact with me. I look back at my young patient's distracted face.

"Okay, bud, let me take you to your room and then Dad and I can talk," I say, making sure we're in agreement.

"I don't know why you guys don't just talk in front of me. I'm not stupid and I'm not five years old anymore," he looks up at me and sighs.

"No, you're not stupid. Who else could complete a one thousand piece puzzle in under an hour? I promise we will soon enough but there are a few things that your dad and I have to discuss. We'll be right in, bud," I say as I lead him into his hospital room.

"I do puzzles in an hour because there's nothing to do, other than count the ceiling tiles and I've already done it three times," he says, jumping into his bed.

I motion to the depressed father that we should talk a little further down the hallway, where no one could hear his worries.

"Um.. so I'm really not sure how I'm gonna pay for this yet. I haven't spoken to his grandparents or really anyone. Whatever I have to do, I'll do it. I just need him to get better," the dad instinctively says and I hear his voice crack more with each word.

"We don't need to talk about that right now. Let's just focus on getting a smile on your little boy's face. I just wanted to give you a chance to let your emotions out, where no one needs to see."

"Thank you, I just - please please just make him better," he says sobbing.

"That is my one and only concern, I promise you."

I sat with him and let him finish crying, without protest, for what felt like hours.

I walk through the never ending hallway once again and feel a throbbing pain in my head. I see the room spin but this time I notice myself falling to the ground.

"Screw you, I knew you couldn't focus on your family for more than two seconds. I knew you would leave us again. How old is she this time?" I hear my mother shout, fighting with my father once again, as I feel my head pound as if it's about to explode.

I'm back on the ground and feel physically incapable of getting up. I hear my mother scream my name multiple times but I can't see her.

I wake up, once again, in a hospital bed. It looks as though they've done some construction but maybe they've just cleaned a little. I jump out of the bed and feel myself yanked back, hitting my head on the edge of the bed. Now, my head throbs from the concussion I've likely given myself, as I stare at the IV's in my arms.

"Adelaide, are you okay? You're still a little drowsy, the doctor said you have to lie down."

"What? Mom, why are you here?"

"I know we don't get along, Adelaide but I'm the one who brought you here."

"What? You're not making any sense. I'm supposed to be the doctor," I say as I notice someone in a similar lab coat walk into my room.

"She hasn't been taking her Adderall?"

"What are you even talking about? I've never seen you here before," I shout at this know-it-all.

"You've never been here before, Adelaide," my mom forces me to sit back in the bed, "so to answer that question, I guess not. I saw the box she keeps her pills in was empty but I swore she had another bottle."

"I'll write up another prescription but this one will be stronger so she has less of these episodes."

"No, I don't want to be here. I'm not taking those pills anymore," I say, knowing that the stronger the medication is, the less I can escape.

The Game of "No"

The word "no" became almost a game to me. After hearing it constantly, I became almost intrigued by it; I wanted to see just how many I could get. I knew the answer to most of the questions I asked, but I started to become just a little anxious when it came to life changing questions.

"Can I have the papers to emancipate myself?" I was at my wit's end. This was one of those big picture moments, the one thing that could get me away from foster hell.

"Age?" the woman at the courthouse didn't even bother looking up from her Sudoku.

"Well, I'm 15, but I'm mature for my age, and I have a job and-" she didn't even let me finish.

"The state of Illinois requires a minor requesting emancipation to be 16. You're going to have to wait. Next!" She knew she couldn't help me, so she didn't even take a moment to apologize for it. I guess a certain "no" can hurt worse than the others.

"None of you ungrateful Annie wannabe's will help me with the groceries?" the wicked witch of foster care shouted through the house. She could never do anything herself; we had to bring in her groceries, but God forbid we ate any.

"If we're Annie, then she's Miss Hannigan," George, my foster brother, whispers to me. He always brings some sort of life into our situation; he's the only one I'd really miss when I leave. I let out a little chuckle as we ran to the door to bring in the groceries.

"Ungrateful brats," my foster mother shouts, pretending it's under her breath.

After the five of us put away the groceries, my foster sister and I ran into our room before our evil foster mother could make us do anything else. I share a room with two other girls and they are not in the least bit neat, so when it's time for our weekly room checks, I'm always stuck deep cleaning the pigsty.

"Lily, can you pass me the paper? Lily!" my annoying foster sister shouts any time she wants someone's attention. She can never do anything for herself.

"Get it yourself! What's wrong with you?" I don't have the time for her entitled little attitude.

"Okay, Lily. Gosh, you don't have to be mean about it," she says in her little victim voice.

The word "no" became my lifestyle; it would be said multiple times a day in one way or another. If it wasn't being told to me, then it would be said by me. I've gotten sick and tired of the millions of kids coming in and out of this house and finally decided to not even attempt to learn who they are. George is the absolute only exception to my rule.

At night it became a game between me and George to scavenge for food and attempt to hang out after lights out. My evil foster mother barely lets us talk to the people in our room, let alone the rest of the kids here. George is a genius, so we can't even socialize in school; this is our only option.

"What'chu got?" George whispers from the pantry.

"Not much," I frown as I hold up the snack pack of fruit snacks.

"I think I hit the jackpot, Lily," George smirks and holds up a family-sized bag of Cheetos.

"Don't you think she'll notice?" I say, anxious I'll get moved away from George again.

"Lil, there's like eighty other people in this house," He heads straight to the back room.

I instantly backed down and practically flew to the back room. When we were together, I was always down for anything; I appreciated his presence more than anyone else's. We would just talk about the small things; we never bothered to drown each other in more sorrows. The only "bad" things we'd talk about were our crush not liking us or someone not noticing how great we are. We didn't have to talk about the big stuff; we already knew what the other was going through because we had been through it too. We usually spend about two hours in the back room just laughing and catching up.

The next day, my foster sister's alarm went off at five in the morning. Instead of jail time for what I would do to her, I decided to go for a run. We weren't supposed to go out, but our foster witch never checked on us or anything so we come and go as we please for the most part. I ran for an hour and a half just around the neighborhood when an idea jumped into my head. My older brother had to be about nineteen or twenty by now. If I could just find him, then I know he would let me live with him. This began my final search for the way out of foster hell.

My brother and I used to be inseparable, but after our mom left and our dad went to jail, we went into foster care. A few times they would try to keep us together, but eventually my brother got too old, and they decided we were too much trouble to keep together. My brother went into a group home and I've been bouncing around in the system ever since.

I decided to start by simply searching his name, but I knew that would be a bust. If there's one thing our mother taught us, it was never to use our real names. She would always say, "that's how they find you", but now I wish I could find him.

"Lily, what are you doing? Take out the garbage. How many times do I have to tell you to do the same thing? Are you dumb or deaf?" my evil foster mother screamed from outside my doorway.

I immediately closed the tab and searched up "where to buy alcohol underage." I knew that she would check the computer after I left, but she wouldn't believe that I was just looking up puppies or something. If I wanted to hide my trail - and I needed to - then I would have to make it believable.

After months of scarching, I became more and more depressed and felt hopeless. What made things even worse, was that my one savior in this house was leaving. His mother would get out of rehab and grab him immediately, against her therapist's wishes. Once she couldn't handle him anymore, she would ruin her life all over again and go straight back to rehab, making George feel like he lost her again every time. Therefore, I knew he would be back, but I hoped that I wouldn't be here much longer so I said a final goodbye. George was confused and concerned as to why I was crying; I never told him, I figured that I would spare his feelings until it actually happened.

After about a month, George came back and since I found where my brother was staying, I decided to explain the situation to him.

"Wait, why didn't you ever tell me you had a brother?" George looked shocked.

"It was always too painful to talk about. It just sucks being separated from your best friend and the one person that knows everything about you," I pulled up the address on the slow computer in the back room that we share with everyone else in the house.

"That's like three hours away. How are you gonna get there?" George stared at me.

"I don't know but it could be worse," I told him, looking hopeful.

"Yeah, I guess."

George never liked to get his hopes up about anything, especially about getting out of the system. I however, am not wired that way. I tried to just relax and act as though it wasn't happening but if any foster kid was in my situation and had a one-way ticket out, I'm sure they'd be just as excited.

After three weeks of working and saving up, I finally had enough money for a bus ticket out. I packed up all of my things in my ripped duffle bag and decided on leaving tonight.

"Are you sure you won't come with me?" I pleaded one last time.

"Lil, I can't. We don't even know if he has room for you, let alone-"

"He'll make room for me, I know he will."

"I know Lily, but I doubt he'll have room for me too," George backed down.

"Say goodbye to me before I leave?" I asked George, the only person I told.

"Course."

At twelve at night, I snuck into the back room with my bag ready.

George and I decided on having one last hangout before I left. We talked for two hours and we cried for one of them. I never thought I would think twice about leaving this place, but I never knew I would meet George.

I threw my bag over my shoulder and quietly ran out the back door. I sprinted to the bus station and bought a one-way ticket to Iowa. I slept the whole way there and only woke up to the bus driver telling me it's time to leave. I had to walk the rest of the way but it was only a mile away from the bus station.

When I finally saw 349, my jaw dropped. The apartment building looked rich but he could be in the worst apartment, who knows? Knowing his favorite alias, I rang the bell for Johnson and waited to be let up. He didn't seem to be home but some woman was coming out of the building and politely held the door open for me - I wasn't going to pass up on that opportunity. I slipped into the elevator and went straight to his apartment. I knocked on the door but when a woman answered, I could feel my heart sink. At that moment, I knew everything I had worked for was gone, but I still decided to try.

"Is there by any chance a man that lives here?" I asked, full of hope.

"Yes, my husband is out right now. How do you know him?" the gorgeous woman with a baby on her hip asked.

"Oh, um… I don't exactly know that I do but I'm looking for my brother. It's a complicated story but do you mind if I wait for your husband? Just in case there's any way he could be my brother, or know where my brother is, I would love to just talk to him. I can wait in the hallway if you want."

"No, you can come in. I'm Sarah, it's nice to meet you."

"I'm Lily."

"Seriously?" Sarah looked shocked.

"Yeah, why?" I felt even more surprised than her.

"Well, that's my daughter's name. My husband actually named her," she smiled at me.

I had no clue what to say so I just sat down and waited. Sarah attempted to make some small talk but I was too anxious to see if I came all the way here for nothing. Then, I heard keys in the door and I felt my heart racing.

"Hi babe, I'm h-" a man shouted from the door, "Wait, Lily? Lily, is that you?"

"Yeah, it's me," I ran into a bear hug and felt instant relief.

"How have you been?"

"Well, awful really, but I'm good now that you're here."

"I can't believe you found me, Lil," he looked at Sarah, almost searching for her approval.

"Yeah. Um… I wanted to talk to you about something. Do you mind if I-" I didn't get to finish.

"Can we talk outside?" he motioned to the door.

Once we got outside, I decided to start again, "Do you mind if I stay with you for a little while? I can't emancipate myself yet and everything's terrible there I just don't know what to do."

"Lil, I have a family. It costs so much to raise-" he kept looking at the floor.

"I know, but I promise I wouldn't be a burden. I can pay rent, I can-" I got interrupted once again.

"Lil, I wish I could but I don't have any room right now. I can help you find a place tomorrow, you can stay until then."

"I don't have enough money for that. Where would a fifteen year old get enough money for an apartment?" I started getting angrier with each word he spoke.

"We'll figure something out, Lily."

"So I can't stay with you?"

This was the last time I ever used the word "no" as a game. This word was something that could break my heart and cause me to lose every reason for working and providing clothes and food for myself.

"I'm sorry Lily. I love you, but no."

Overachieving Student Underachieving at Self-Love

Julie jumps off of her bed and gently smooths over the indent she just made. She walks over to her crystal clear mirror and stares at her reflection. Her eyes flutter to her hair as she combs her fingers through.

"Perfect," Julie declares as she smirks. She glances at her phone; 5:20 AM. She had been up for almost an hour now, going over her study materials for her math test today. She calmly walks to the kitchen table and grabs her backpack. She unzips the front and pulls out a neatly packed folder that says, "STUDY MATERIALS." She opens the folder and begins to look over each paper carefully, paying extra attention to her study guide.

Julie glances at the clock and it ticks to 6:45 AM. She carefully repacks her backpack and swings it over her shoulder while heading out the front door. She walks to the bus stop and sees a short blonde-haired girl walking from the other direction.

"Julie! I'm starving. You wanna come grab a bagel before first period?" Laylah, her best friend asks.

"Can't. Gotta study," Julie replies with a small apologetic smile as the bus pulls up.

"You'll never take your nose out of those damn books, huh?" Laylah sighs, shaking her head.

Julie ignores the comment and gets on the bus. Instantly, she unzips her backpack and gets back to work.

"Hun, this is your stop," the bus driver prompts Julie to get off the bus. Julie looks around at the empty seats and quickly, but carefully, stuffs all of her papers back into her backpack.

"Sorry, sorry," Julie apologizes as she rushes off of the bus and heads straight to the library.

BRRRING. Julie looks up at the clock, "No, no, no," she looks at her scattered papers on the library table and sighs.

In Julie's fifth period class, Julie opens up her study materials, once again, and frantically rushes over each page. Math class is already bad enough without having to take a test. At least she only had one more class before lunch, she hadn't eaten all day and she could feel her stomach grumbling. Ms. Finn, the math teacher, asks her to put away her papers and passes out the tests. She continuously shakes her leg until she is handed the test. She takes a deep breath and looks down at the first page. She stares at the first question for five minutes before putting her pen down on the paper. She boxes every answer neatly, showing her work in perfect columns. She is only about halfway through her test when she hears "pencils down".

"No, no, no. This can't be happening," Julie looks down at her test with wide eyes and begins shaking her leg once more, but faster, feeling her chest constrict and her heart thumping. When the teacher comes around to collect her test she pleads, "Please, please let me finish, Ms. Finn. I can do it, I promise. I studied so much for this test. Please."

Ms. Finn looks at her for a moment before lightly smiling. "Okay fine, but you'll have to come back during lunch."

"Yes, yes, thank you," Julie says with every ounce of gratitude she can muster as she scrambles to her next class.

Julie was so drained from her math test that she fell asleep during her next class. When the bell rang, she jolted upright, realizing what she had done, and apologized profusely to her teacher. The teacher understood that this was out of character for Julie, and permitted her to do her work at home and submit it the next day. She packed up her backpack, still neatly, but in a quicker fashion this time.

"Yo, late again, Jules," Laylah meets Julie at the classroom door, "what did your mom pack for us today?"

Julie giggles and hands Laylah her brown paper bag, "You can have it, I have to finish my math test."

"What?" Laylah looks at her with concern, "You should at least eat part of this."

"I know, but I have to make sure everything's right. I struggled so badly with the last half so Ms. Finn told me I could have extra time."

"Fine, I'll just eat alone, again," Laylah sighs, and walks to the cafeteria while Julie walks to her math classroom. Before entering, she takes a deep breath.

"Okay, Julie, time's up," Ms. Finn comes over to Julie's desk.

"Wait, wait, please can I have one more second? I just wanna look over this question one more time,"

Julie begs, not even looking up from her exam.

"It's not gonna be perfect, hun, and the bell is going to ring. You'll have to get to class."

Julie reluctantly hands Ms. Finn her paper, swings her backpack over her shoulder, and leaves the classroom. She looks down at her watch and realizes she used all of her lunch hour for this test. As if in reply, her stomach lets out a loud rumbling noise.

"Just wait until 6, just wait until dinner," Julie whispers while looking down at her stomach, knowing that food is strictly prohibited in her afternoon classes.

Julie and 10 other students pile onto the bus. As soon as she sits down, Julie grabs her homework from her bag and writes furiously on the paper.

"Alright kid, this is it," Julie looks up at the bus driver motioning for her to leave. Julie packs up her papers and jumps up.

Julie rushes into her house and frantically sprawls out her homework on the kitchen table. She furiously writes for two hours until she has yawned so much that she gives in and takes a nap.

"Jules! Julie! You gotta get to work!" Julie's mom exclaims while shaking her awake.

"Oh no," Julie glares at the clock and barely has enough time to throw her hair up. On the ride to work, Julie's stomach growls blaringly, "ugh," Julie exclaims and glances down at her stomach and whispers, "when I get home."

Julie rushes into work and smiles at every person passing by. Julie looks at the clock every five minutes throughout her entire shift. When the work is light, she mentally goes over her vocabulary words. She can tell that it's almost closing time because the lights always dim 30 minutes before. She notices the lights dimming faster and faster. She starts packing up the supplies and thinking of all the classes she needs to study for. Suddenly, the lights go completely black.

"Julie? Julie!" Her coworkers rush towards her as she falls to the ground. Minutes later, an ambulance arrives and rushes Julie to the hospital.

"Julie?" her mom asks as she opens her eyes, "Julie, honey, you fainted and the doctors say-"

"Where's my homework?" Julie mumbles.

"What?" Her mother asks, astonished.

"My homework, or my study materials, I need them."

"You need to take a break, Jules."

Ignoring her mother, Julie springs up out of the hospital bed, "no, Mom. I need them," Julie notices the lights going out, and once again, she's on the floor.

Chilling Truth of Family

"Don't ask for a thing when we get in the store. You don't deserve anything. Make sure you worthless animals are under control or I will gladly show you just how angry I am when we get home." He growls at the kids, but I know those words were directed at me as well. I stare at the ground like always. I can never look at them or I know I won't be able to handle myself, as I know the words are stinging my children the more he speaks. However, I am numb to him. His words. His lies. His tricks. His anger. His forcefulness. His beatings. I just strive to keep my children and I alive day by day.

"You're so cute!" A woman pokes and prods my daughter. I glare at her because I know what's coming next. My daughter screams. I wince. She runs to the back of the store and I lose track of her. No no no no no. This isn't happening. Why couldn't this woman mind her own business?

"Thank you so much! I'm so sorry I need to go find where my daughter went. I don't know why she's acting like this. I apologize again." He has always been such a smooth talker. He is the sweetest man alive to everyone, except us, but no one would ever know that.

Left foot. Right foot. One in front of the other. Don't look behind. Don't speak to anyone. I hope she ran into a kidnapper. That would be a chance to get away from his grip. I don't want this life for her. She could and should be so much more.

There she is. Tears running down her face. She knows she messed up. She knows what's coming next. My five year old son stares up at me for reassurance. For the first time, I look back at him. He has the most precious blue eyes. I wonder if I have blue eyes. I haven't seen a mirror in decades. We don't have mirrors at the house. I'm not even allowed in public bathrooms, in case I try to sneak a peek. Even if someone takes out a compact, I have to make sure to look away or I'll get an extra beating when I get home. I should've never locked eyes with my son. Looking at him kills me. I can't give him the reassurance he needs. I'm a coward. I dream of slitting that man's throat while he sleeps - that is, if he ever lets me out of the basement at night. It's better that I can't though, if I ever tried anything, I know he would make my kids pay. Even if I succeeded, his father knows our exact situation and is even worse. I draw my eyes back to the floor and pick a spot to stare at.

"Oh just wait til we get home," he says so calmly.

I know she's fighting back tears. I can feel her pain. I don't want to live like this anymore, but I can't save her now. That was her third strike.

Later at the house, my husband grabs my daughter by the hair and yanks her down those ugly old stairs to the basement. He takes three steps down himself and throws her the rest of the way. I hear his footsteps coming back up the stairs and I know what he wants. My five year old son runs as quick as any person ever has and squeezes me so tight. I kiss him and then throw him off because I know if my husband ever found him like that we would all be down in the basement. He would not hear of a weak son. Because of this, I know my beautiful baby boy will be beating on me one day. The last stair creaks on his way up to meet me in the kitchen.

"Let's go," he demands me into the basement. I immediately run over as I know if I don't I will be thrown ten times as hard as my daughter.

"I'll be back. No use doing anything until she wakes up," he calmly states as I bring my eyes over to my daughter who is passed out on the ground, "don't forget - I know everything. Try anything and tonight will be your last." Oh how I wish tonight was my last night, but I know he enjoys it too much. Every time he lays a hand on me, he laughs. He gets so much joy from it. He would never let me go.

"Mom?" I know this means he'll be here soon.

"Don't say anything. He's listening." I know I'll be reprimanded for this.

The loudest creak I've ever heard a stair make just came from the top of the steps. Instantly my daughter winces, as she always does before a beating, and this makes me realize he hasn't ruined her yet. She thinks she is only getting another beating. She doesn't know he wants to take away her innocence before anyone else can. It's not too late for her.

I rush to the tool box my husband keeps. He knows I am too afraid to use any tools so he leaves it unlocked. Today I gained my courage. He will not ruin my daughter like he did me. I hear the creak of the second step. I grab the sharpest screwdriver I could find. I sprint back over to my daughter and I know this is it. This is the end.

He is at the bottom of the stairs now. I kiss my daughter on the top of her head as I jam the screwdriver through her heart.

"I'm sorry my angel, this is the only way." He would not get to ruin her.

"You're fucking kidding me," he screams at me and I know I won.